SUPER SIMPLE BODY

INSIDE THE BONES

KARIN HALVORSON, M.D.

Consulting Editor, Diane Craig, M.A./Reading Specialist

Super Sandcastle

An Imprint of Abdo Publishing
abdopublishing.com

VISIT US AT ABDOPUBLISHING.COM

Published by Abdo Publishing, a division of ABDO, PO Box 398166, Minneapolis, Minnesota 55439. Copyright © 2016 by Abdo Consulting Group, Inc. International copyrights reserved in all countries. No part of this book may be reproduced in any form without written permission from the publisher. Super SandCastle™ is a trademark and logo of Abdo Publishing.

Printed in the United States of America,
North Mankato, Minnesota
102015
012016

THIS BOOK CONTAINS RECYCLED MATERIALS

Editor: Liz Salzmann
Content Developer: Nancy Tuminelly
Cover and Interior Design: Mighty Media, Inc.
Photo Credits: Shutterstock

Library of Congress Cataloging-in-Publication Data
Halvorson, Karin, 1979- author.
  Inside the bones / Karin Halvorson, M.D. ; consulting editor, Diane Craig, M.A./reading specialist.
    pages cm. -- (Super simple body)
  ISBN 978-1-62403-939-3
1. Bones--Juvenile literature. 2. Skeleton--Juvenile literature. I. Title. II. Series: Halvorson, Karin, 1979- Super simple body.
  QP88.2.H325 2016
  612.7'5--dc23
                          2015020616

Super SandCastle™ books are created by a team of professional educators, reading specialists, and content developers around five essential components—phonemic awareness, phonics, vocabulary, text comprehension, and fluency—to assist young readers as they develop reading skills and strategies and increase their general knowledge. All books are written reviewed, and leveled for guided reading and early reading intervention programs for use in shared, guided, and independent reading and writing activities to support a balanced approach to literacy instruction.

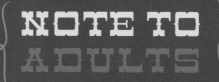

{NOTE TO ADULTS}

THIS BOOK is all about encouraging children to learn the science of how their bodies work! Be there to help make science fun and interesting for young readers. Many activities are included in this book to help children further explore what they've learned. Some require adult assistance and/or permission. Make sure children have appropriate places where they can do the activities safely.

Children may also have questions about what they've learned. Offer help and guidance when they have questions. Most of all, encourage them to keep exploring and learning new things!

CONTENTS

YOUR BODY

YOUR BONES

You're amazing! So is your body!
Your body has a lot of different parts. Your **kidneys**, skin, blood, muscles, and bones all work together every day. They keep you moving. Even when you don't realize it.

Your body needs bones! They give your body a basic shape. They keep the organs in your body safe. The insides of your bones make blood cells.

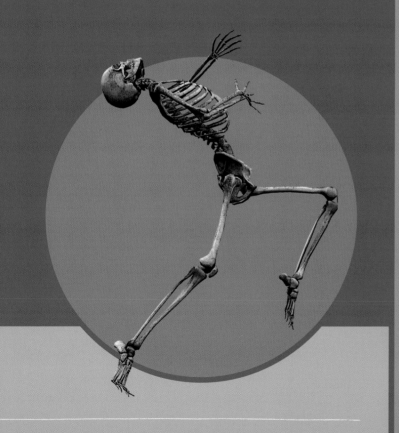

BONE
BEGINNINGS

Bones start as cartilage (*KAHR-tuh-lij*). Cartilage is soft and bendable. **Calcium** sticks to the cartilage. The cartilage hardens. It becomes bone.

Babies have more than 300 bones. Adults have 206 bones. Some bones **fuse** together as they grow.

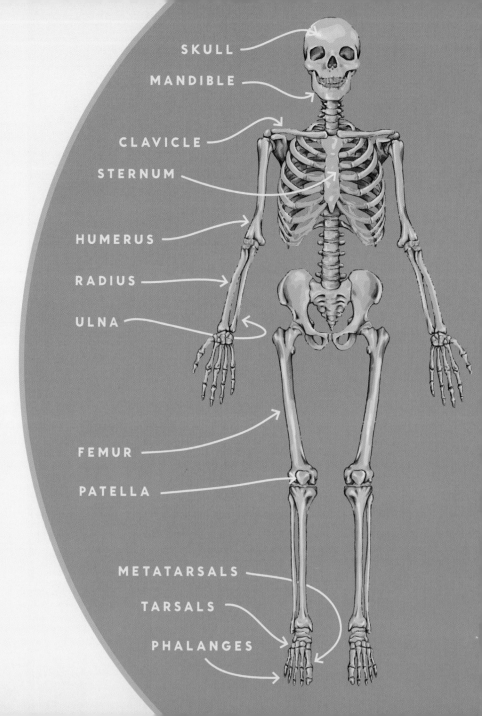

SKULL

MANDIBLE

CLAVICLE

STERNUM

HUMERUS

RADIUS

ULNA

FEMUR

PATELLA

METATARSALS

TARSALS

PHALANGES

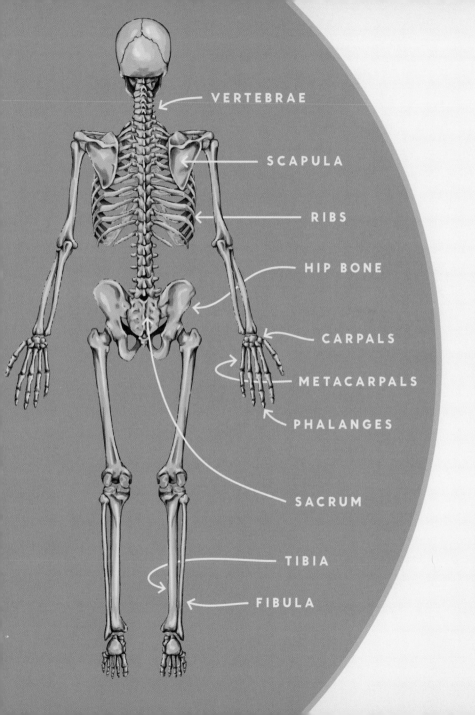

VERTEBRAE

SCAPULA

RIBS

HIP BONE

CARPALS

METACARPALS

PHALANGES

SACRUM

TIBIA

FIBULA

X-Ray Photos

Doctors can take pictures of bones. These pictures are called x-rays. They help doctors see what's happening inside your body.

Have you had an x-ray?

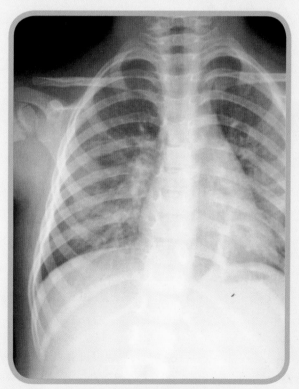

A CHEST X-RAY

A BLANKET
FOR YOUR BONES

The periosteum (*per-ee-OS-tee-uhm*) is a thin layer of **tissue**. It covers your bones. It keeps your **nerves** and blood vessels in place. Your bones get minerals from your nerves and blood vessels. The periosteum helps your bones grow strong!

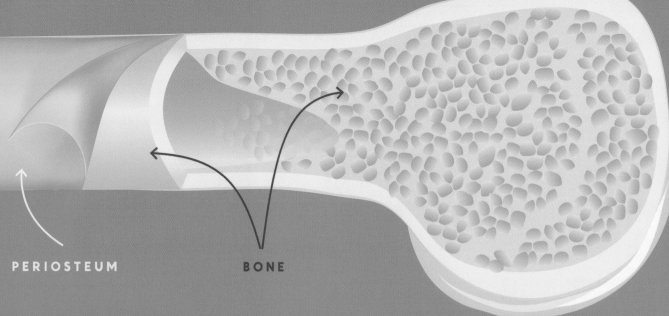

PERIOSTEUM

BONE

Your **nerves** send sensory signals to your brain. They tell you how your bones feel.

The blood vessels are like highways. They move blood to and from your bones.

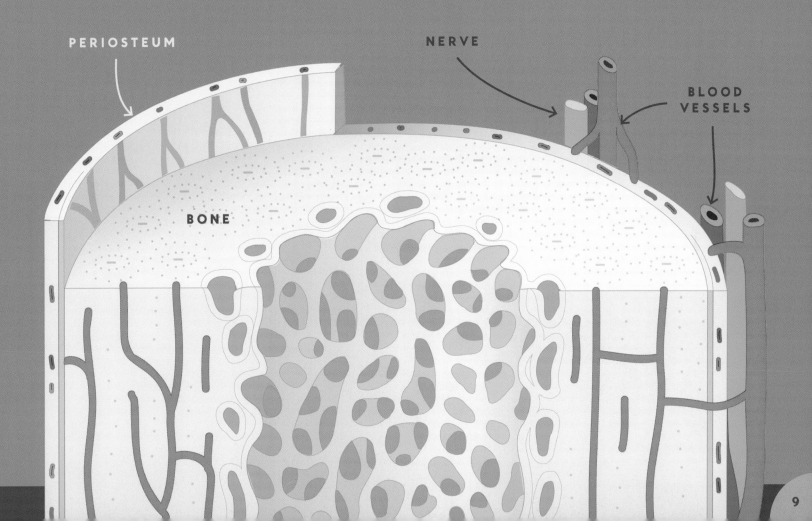

PERIOSTEUM

NERVE

BLOOD VESSELS

BONE

COMPACT
BONE

The outer part of a bone is white and hard. It has a smooth surface. It's called compact bone.

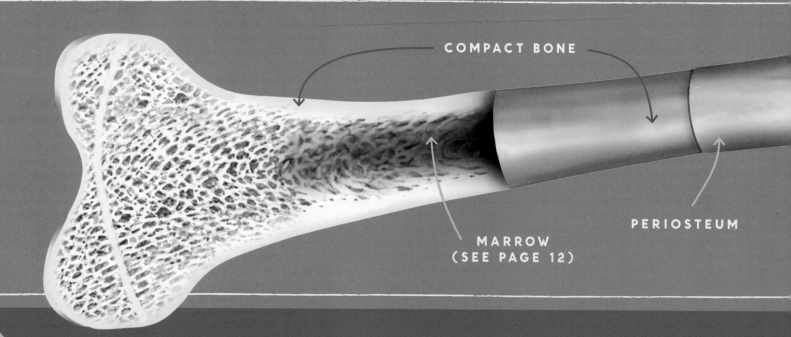

COMPACT BONE

PERIOSTEUM

MARROW
(SEE PAGE 12)

SPONGY
BONE

The inner part of a bone is called spongy bone. It looks like a sponge. It is full of holes. It is also soft. Spongy bone stores **calcium**. It makes the bone strong.

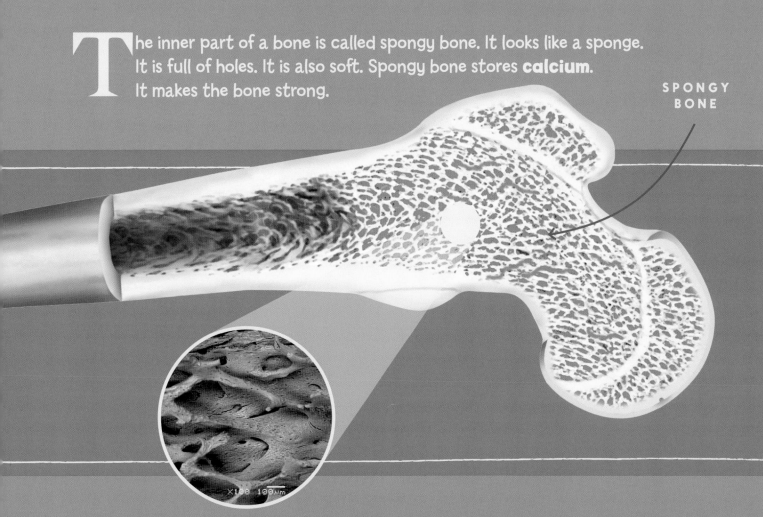

SPONGY BONE

X100 100µm

MARROW

BONE MARROW sits in the holes of the spongy bone. It's soft and squishy, like jelly.

Red or Yellow?

There are two types of bone marrow. Red bone marrow makes blood cells. Yellow bone marrow stores fat.

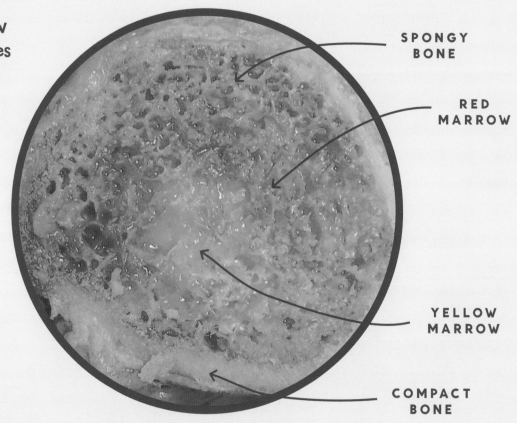

SPONGY BONE

RED MARROW

YELLOW MARROW

COMPACT BONE

INSIDE A BONE

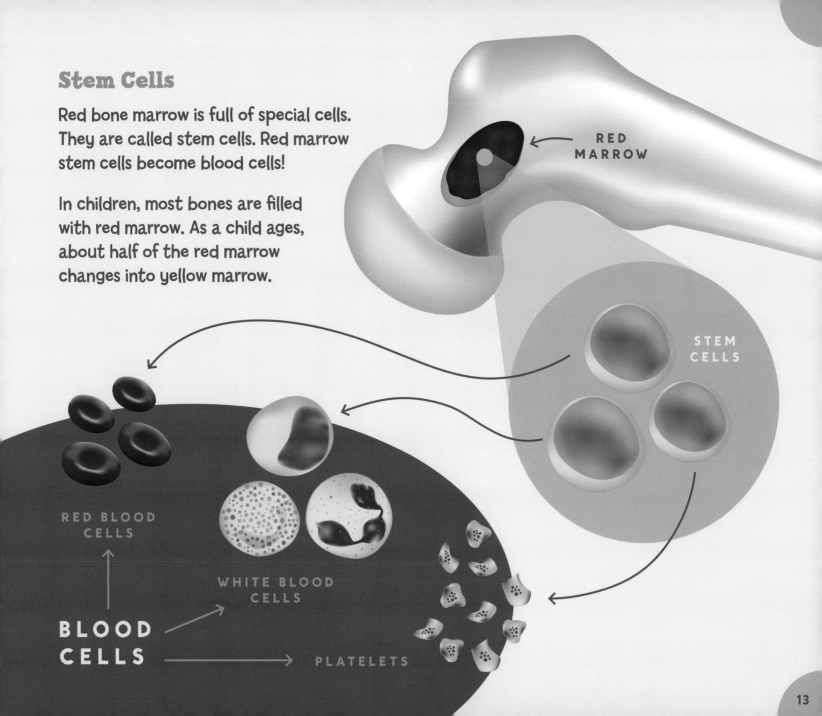

Stem Cells

Red bone marrow is full of special cells. They are called stem cells. Red marrow stem cells become blood cells!

In children, most bones are filled with red marrow. As a child ages, about half of the red marrow changes into yellow marrow.

RED MARROW

STEM CELLS

RED BLOOD CELLS

WHITE BLOOD CELLS

BLOOD CELLS

PLATELETS

A FUNNY BONE

MAKE YOUR OWN BONE!

WHAT YOU NEED: **WHITE CLAY, RED CHENILLE STEM, THIN SPONGE, TOILET PAPER TUBE, RED TISSUE PAPER, CRAFT GLUE**

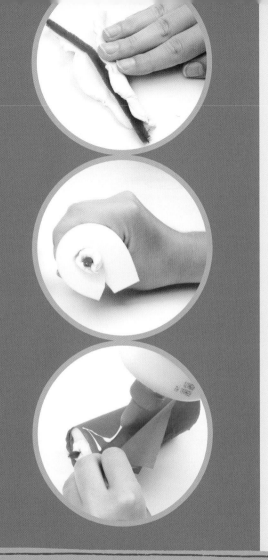

HOW TO DO IT

1. Roll clay around the chenille stem.

2. Wrap the sponge around the clay.

3. Fit the sponge inside the tube.

4. Wrap the red **tissue** paper around the tube. Glue it in place.

WHAT'S HAPPENING?

The clay is the bone marrow. The chenille stem is a stem cell. The sponge is the spongy bone. The tube is the compact bone. The tissue paper is the periosteum.

BODY ARMOR

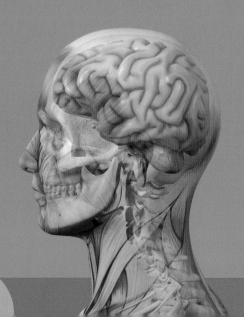

Bones give your body a shape. They also keep important parts of your body safe. Your skull protects your brain. You can feel your skull. It is under the hair on your head.

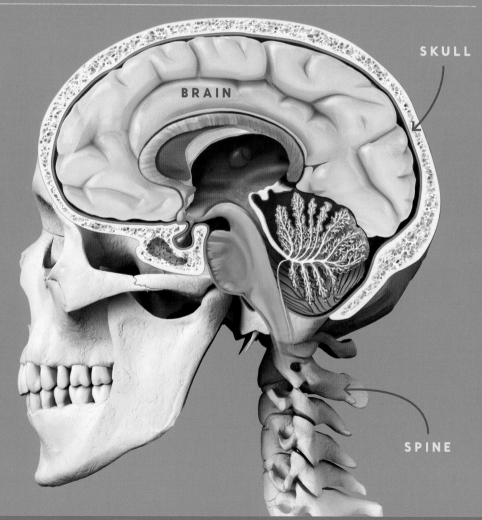

BRAIN

SKULL

SPINE

Your spine is bone too. It keeps your spinal cord safe. You can feel your spine. The bumps in the middle of your back make up your spine!

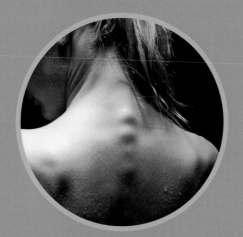

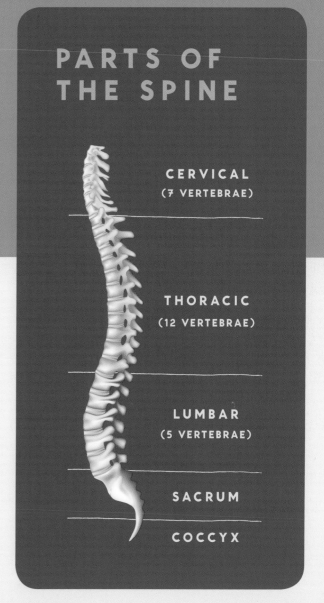

CERVICAL
(7 VERTEBRAE)

THORACIC
(12 VERTEBRAE)

LUMBAR
(5 VERTEBRAE)

SACRUM

COCCYX

SPINAL CORD

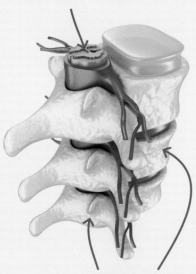

Your spine is made up of small bones. They are called vertebrae (*vur-tuh-BRAY*). Adults have 24 vertebrae plus the sacrum and the coccyx.

VERTEBRAE

GROW A SPINE

SEE HOW YOUR SPINE WORKS!

HOW TO DO IT

1. Cut the cups of the egg carton apart.

2. Punch holes on opposite sides of each cup.

3. Press the holes together to flatten the cups.

4. Twist the chenille stems together.

5. Thread the stems through the holes in the cups.

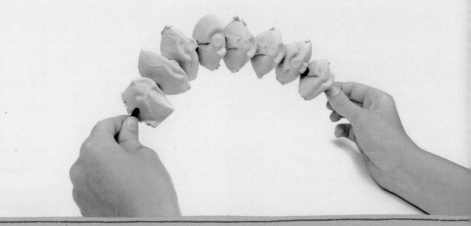

WHAT'S HAPPENING?

The egg carton cups are the vertebrae. The chenille stems are the spinal cord. The vertebrae keep the spinal cord safe and let it bend.

THE RIBS

Your ribs are important bones. They protect your lungs and heart.

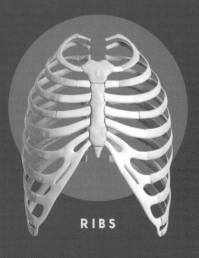

RIBS

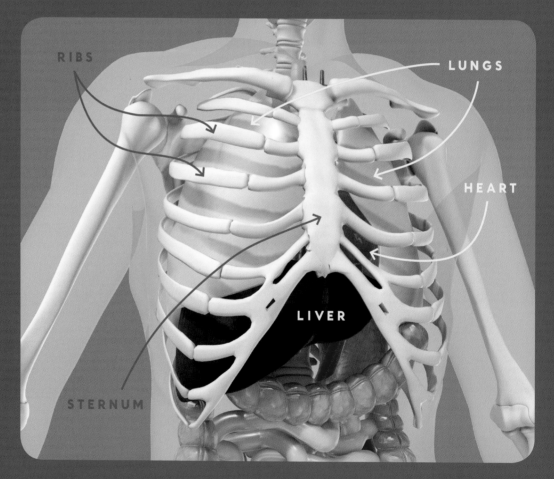

RIBS

LUNGS

HEART

LIVER

STERNUM

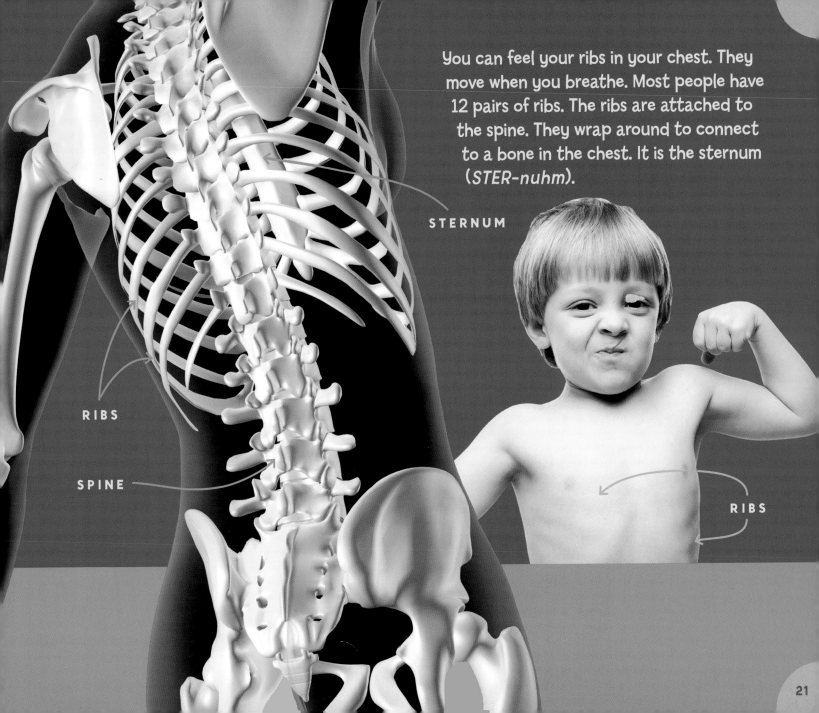

You can feel your ribs in your chest. They move when you breathe. Most people have 12 pairs of ribs. The ribs are attached to the spine. They wrap around to connect to a bone in the chest. It is the sternum (*STER-nuhm*).

STERNUM

RIBS

SPINE

RIBS

ARMS & HANDS

Your arms help you do things. You use them to eat. You also use them to brush your teeth. Each arm has three bones.

The humerus (*HYOO-muh-ruhs*) connects the shoulder to the elbow. The radius (*RAY-dee-uhs*) and ulna (*UHL-nuh*) connect the elbow to the hand.

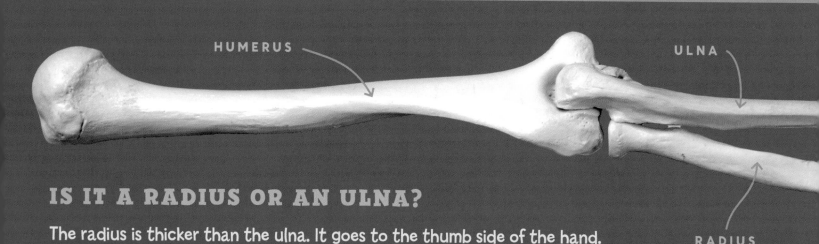

HUMERUS

ULNA

RADIUS

IS IT A RADIUS OR AN ULNA?

The radius is thicker than the ulna. It goes to the thumb side of the hand.

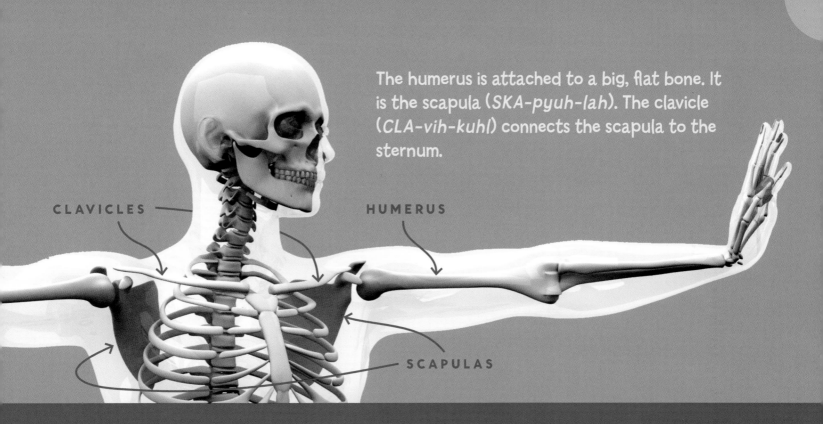

The humerus is attached to a big, flat bone. It is the scapula (*SKA-pyuh-lah*). The clavicle (*CLA-vih-kuhl*) connects the scapula to the sternum.

CLAVICLES

HUMERUS

SCAPULAS

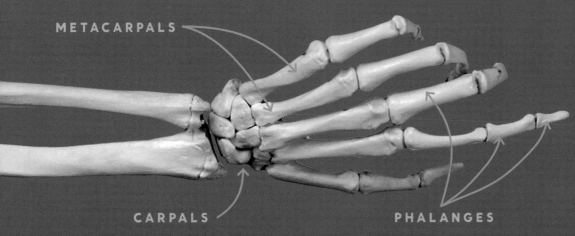

METACARPALS

CARPALS

PHALANGES

Your hands have many small bones. Some are carpals (*CAR-puhlz*). Others are metacarpals (*met-uh-CAR-puhlz*). The finger bones are phalanges (*fuh-LAN-jeez*).

BENDY BONES

MAKE YOUR BONES MELT!

WHAT YOU NEED: CLEAN DRY CHICKEN BONE, DRINKING GLASS, VINEGAR, PAPER TOWEL

HOW TO DO IT

1. Try to bend the bone. Don't force it too hard! You don't want to break it.

2. Fill a glass with vinegar. Put the bone in the vinegar. Leave it there for 3 days.

3. Pour the vinegar out. Refill the glass with new vinegar. Leave the bone in the vinegar for 2 more days.

4. Take the bone out of the glass. Dry it off. Try to bend it.

WHAT'S HAPPENING?

There is **calcium** in bones. The calcium keeps the bone from bending. The vinegar breaks down the calcium. Then the bone can bend.

LEGS & FEET

Your legs get you from one place to another. Your legs are attached to your hip bones. Each leg has four bones.

The femur (*FEE-mer*) connects the hip to the knee. The tibia (*TIB-ee-uh*) and fibula (*FIB-yuh-luh*) connect the knee to the foot.

A special bone keeps the knee safe. It is the patella (*puh-TEL-uh*). It is also called the kneecap.

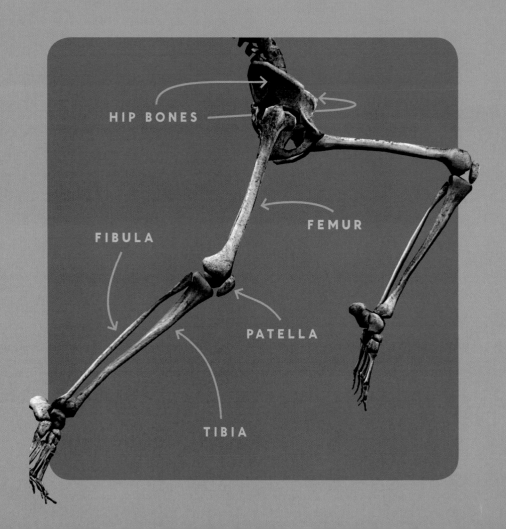

HIP BONES

FEMUR

FIBULA

PATELLA

TIBIA

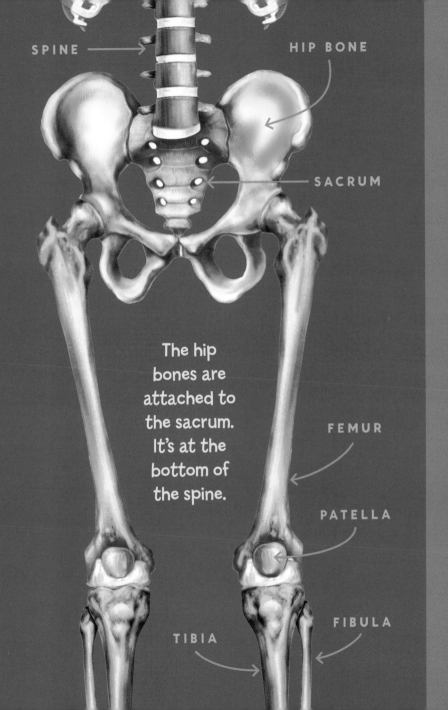

SPINE

HIP BONE

SACRUM

The hip bones are attached to the sacrum. It's at the bottom of the spine.

FEMUR

PATELLA

TIBIA

FIBULA

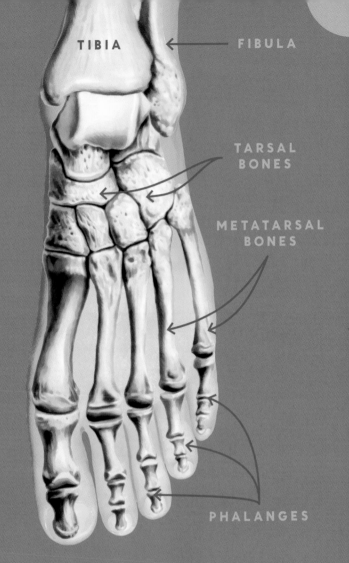

TIBIA

FIBULA

TARSAL BONES

METATARSAL BONES

PHALANGES

There are many small bones in your feet. Toe bones are called phalanges. Just like finger bones!

CHIEF JOINTS

A joint is a place where two bones meet. Joints let the body bend and twist. The body has many joints.

Ball and Socket Joints

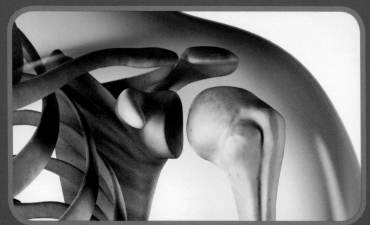

THE SHOULDER JOINT

THE HIP JOINT

Shoulder and Hip

The shoulder and hip are ball-and-**socket** joints. The bones fit together like a baseball and a glove. These joints let you move in many directions.

Elbow and Knee

The elbow and knee are **hinge** joints. They work like the hinge on a door. Hinge joints bend in one direction.

Hinge Joints

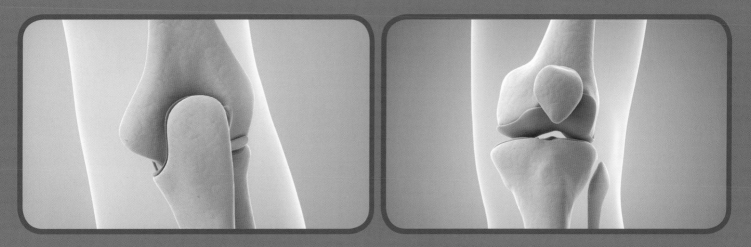

THE ELBOW JOINT

THE KNEE JOINT

SKELE-TONI

MAKE A PASTA SKELETON!

WHAT YOU NEED: PASTA IN DIFFERENT SHAPES, PAPER PLATE, WHITE PAINT, PAINTBRUSH, BLACK TAG BOARD, CRAFT GLUE, WHITE MARKER

HOW TO DO IT

1 Put the pasta shapes on the paper plate. Paint them white. Let the paint dry.

2 Lay the pasta shapes on the tag board. Arrange them in the shape of a skeleton. Glue the shapes in place. Let the glue dry.

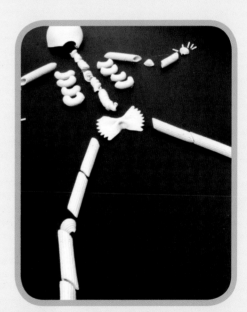

3 Label the bones and joints.

WHAT'S HAPPENING?

You made a pasta skeleton! See how many joints and bones you find and label.

GLOSSARY

CALCIUM – a natural element that is needed for good health, especially for healthy teeth and bones.

FUSE – to become blended together.

HINGE – a joint that allows two attached parts to move.

KIDNEY – an organ in the body that turns waste from the blood into urine.

NERVE – one of the threads in the body that takes messages to and from the brain.

PLATELET – a type of blood cell that helps blood clot.

SOCKET – an opening that holds something, such as a light socket.

TISSUE – 1. a group of similar cells that form one part of a plant or animal. 2. very thin paper.